PLENTY THOUGHTS FROM AN EMPTY BRAIN

THOUGHTS DO NOT HAVE A FORM LIKE THE BRAIN.

ROHAN KOMPELLA

Copyright © Rohan Kompella
All Rights Reserved.

To every part of my brain that made me to think, realize, learn, know about many things from my parents, teachers, friends and from my phone......

Contents

Contents

Preface

'I'NTRODUCTION

• vii •

As said by Karl Marx, "**The circumstances surrounding a man make him**". I believe it's something true. When I was born, I was born with an empty brain and through various stages of life, I started to know, collect, and learn a lot of things with time. "Plenty Thoughts From An Empty Brain" is a conceptual book containing my own thoughts, ideas, and points of view on a wide range of topics and circumstances that I confronted, went through, experienced, observed with, and studied.

"**The object of life is not to be on the side of the majority, but to escape finding oneself in the ranks of the insane**". Marcus Aurelius,

I was never on the side of the majority who believe right or wrong depending on their perspectives and opinions. It's always me being me studying various contexts and concepts, incidents etc.., So the idea for this book is primarily based on my own experiences, research, observations, realizations, thoughts, opinions, and perspectives on a variety of issues, topics, and aspects, as well as various books by Ayn Rand, Friedrich nietzsche,Karl Marx, Hitler, and my friends that have inspired me in various thoughts and contexts to develop myself. It's "I" living my life to the fullest with my thoughts, which and where I pick as a sculpture plucking food from a variety of random food sources available to it, ideologies, opinions, words, phrases, sentences, philosophy, and so on, which I loved and which helped ME to become ME. I've lived my life as I've desired for all of these years, and I'm going to continue to live my life as I've desired..

-Rohan kompella

Acknowledgements

There are persons that helped me in studying numerous and wide topics, which eventually assisted me in learning and improving myself. The movies I watched by skipping maths class, the books I read on the backbench, the people I randomly observed and studied, news articles that informed me about what was going on in the world, and so on, all of these things helped me develop knowledge and learn things better than I could have imagined. As Calvin Cordozar Broadus Jr.'s comments have gone viral: "**Last but not least, I want to thank me, I want to thank me for believing in me.**" So, as of the same case, I'd like to thank myself for assisting myself in learning a lot via the process and progress of maturing, understanding and learning about numerous concepts relevant to various and random things. I'd want to thank myself for believing in myself enough to write this book.

Prologue

"According to this possibly apocryphal story, as Varda was mulling over the threat in the night in the loneliness of the Azad Maidan lockup, he saw an affluent looking man, dressed in a white suit approaching him. The man was smoking a 555 cigarette and exuded a certain calmness.

The man walked up to the iron bars, and not a single one of the cops on duty stopped him.........." lines from one of my favorite books that piqued my interest in books and the manner of writing is something that put me in a trance for writings....

Every book is defined as an art form of expression in which the writer or author expresses his or her thoughts, views, ideas, and other things through lines originating from his or her brain and rearranges them in a logical order so that people can understand them, and at times they are left without rearrangements so that people can pretend to understand them.

So it's the books that we can communicate with people, with the world, with brains of intellectual, intelligents, innocents, idiots, stupids, fools and etc and know whatever you can. It can be 2 pages you can learn a lot and it can be 2 books that can change your whole life's perspective, lifestyle and etc..,

So that's when I finally thought, "Maybe if I can create something like a book with my thoughts, ideas, points of view, and opinions and present it in such a way that someone can read it......"

CHAPTER ONE

My Eyes on Big screen...

"When people ask me if I went to film school I tell them, 'no, I went to films."

- Quentin Tarantino

Cinema was the very first thing I experienced when I became conscious, and it is when I began to adore the concept or phrase "Cinema". My first film was "Vikramarkudu", directed by SS Rajamouli, an Indian film director.

I may have watched random films or movie scenes on television before watching this film, but it was the first film that awakened my attention towards cinema. That was the moment that piqued my interest in cinema. I began to watch random films that were shown on TV at random. It used to be the days where my father used to buy tickets for us and we used to enjoy cinema on "Big screen", at times it used to be the second show on Saturdays of a new release film that results to lazy wake ups on sundays.

Ch. Sarath Chandra, a friend of mine, was the one who initially exposed me to Hollywood films. I used to go to his house, flat no. 206, where we would watch odd heroic films like Superman, Spiderman, and others, and we would play different characters and improve our acting talents with fake deaths.

We used to play a game called Space Ranger, which we created after seeing the movie "Zathura," and we used to arrange pillows as a layout for our spaceship, with him as captain and me as astronaut.

It was back in the 2000s when every morning from 9 a.m. to 12 p.m. and again from 3 p.m. to 6 p.m., a random film would be shown on television. I used to look up the list of films that were going to be broadcasted today in a local newspaper or additional paper on the 14th page and then schedule my off-school time to go home quickly, freshen up, and watch a film.

That piqued my interest in learning about the films that will be broadcast on tv on that specific date.It used to be the Hollywood ones in most cases since, because of my interest in seeing the graphical content of the films, the heroic ones like Spiderman, which was one of my favourite movies, really helped me understand the notion of heroic films in later days. I used to look forward to the school bell ringing so I could go home and watch a random film broadcasted.

I used to jot down the channel numbers of HBO MAX, Star Movies, and other random channels that aired movies on a sheet of paper and glue it to the TV or put the piece of paper in a cabinet adjacent to the TV.

The flims has always helped me deal with the things that happen around me in various and big situations. It's always been the picture I've studied, and it's always been the film that has piqued my interest. I was continuously trying to learn more about films in the settings of new releases, shooting ceremonies, and learning about the cast and crew working and used to differentiate and know the names of the crew, what they are best for, the films they worked on, and so on.

I used to spend more time indoors watching TV than outside playing. My brother and I used to watch local, Hindi, and Hollywood movies. Rather than practising arithmetic, I used to spend my time watching movies. Aside from making excuses or escaping, it has always been my passion that has led me to discover a means to learn about films.

It was the one constant thing I had done in my whole life up to this time. I never used to spend my time in front of my academic books; instead, I'd watch a random film, and I'd thank my mother for allowing me to do so, since my interest in viewing films and learning about them was growing.

My mother used to suggest to me a random old film of different genres, mostly comedy. It was at that moment I started to explore the world of cinema from the 1900's. I used to practice long dialogues of actors with great difficulty and present it to my mother.

She was the one who took me to a theater rather than a tuition center. It was that moment in 2015 that made my watching levels of a film much more interesting and developed my observations while watching cinema, called Bahubali, It was then that I watched a second show, and it was my first experience with going without sleep for an entire night while thinking about a film.

So, apart from my experiences, I spent a lot of time studying films, It is both the same as and not the same as reality. It is the ability of a film that can exist in two places or contexts at the same time. It might be a fictional plot, a sequence, a scene, or a clip claiming to be "far from reality" and the same one claiming to be "near to reality."

CINEMA is something that stays as far as near to the term REALITY.

Whenever I used to watch movies of Steven spilberg and Tarentino, I used to place their books "Shoot like Spielberg" and "Shoot like tarantino" and used to reference out their explanations for the scene or camera techniques and observe them as well.

I used to read a lot of books, watch interviews of film directors and cinematographers which they used to explain the cinema and the way they used to explain a cinema is something that probably made me feel interesting to know more about films.

During my Diploma years, I used to see 2-3 films every week and, on occasion, 2-3 films in a row in a single day. I used to go to threatre after finishing college or when there were strikes that resulted in a holiday and acquire a ticket to a random movie and enjoy myself in that wonderful setting. For me, the theatre known as heaven is more important than the original ones constructed by gods.

As there exist three different terms called FILM, CINEMA and MOVIE and in my personal level, I consider them as, Film is something I believe to be termed as a medium of conveying your story, expression and something you want to show which you believed in.

Movie is something at the same time, term considered for a large scale or known as commercial cinema which and where they target the audience in part and parcel of making money or making a business, often considered as a slang, motion picture.

Cinema is something applied for the whole industry. example.., Indian cinema, Hollywood cinema, Italian cinema etc.., So these three contexts are something I got to understand with time while watching films.

Cinema is my closest companion in my own language and reality. When I am feeling low, I watch a random film and return to my work; when something goes inadvertently well, for example, when I had a decent score in math in my semester exams, I share my unpleasant satisfaction by watching a film at night.

CHAPTER TWO

Age of learning and knowing

"As long as you live, keep learning how to live"

- SENECA

I used to be terrified of learning and trying out new things because I was frightened of the outcome.

- "Will it be all right?"
- "What if things don't go according to plan?"
- "What if I didn't realise?"

"Can I?" and other such questions used to be a roadblock for me in terms of knowing and learning new things, both in school and in real life.

I didn't know how to ride a bicycle until grade two. The reason for this is because the outcome and process I used to be terrified about, for those downfalls or injuries, but my mother was the one who took charge of teaching me how to ride a bicycle and guided me through out the process. It was then that I realized the distinction between the known and the unknown.

Whenever I start something new in learning or vice versa, I remember a quotation by Charlie Munger that says, "You need patience, discipline, and agility to handle losses and adversity without going insane." When I failed several times while learning to ride a bicycle, it was then that I began to ride it effectively and unintentionally, which I now consider lucky. The more I failed, the more I discovered about myself, about my abilities, capabilities and skills which I haven't discovered in my ownself.

"More is lost by indecision than by bad decisions" Marcus Tullius Cicero.

Quotes have always been something that has helped me improve. I believe that one should make a decision about something or anything that allows him to advance in positive or negative ways, regardless of the outcome. All these contexts about learning started from the context of learning to ride a bicycle.

It can be a person thinking to do something or invent something which he believe that it can be a huge success if done but in majority of the cases people stand still in imagination, it's the actions that help you to make your dream work rather than your thoughts in your brain sleeping pleasant along with you.

"Learning never exhausts the mind", Leonardo Da Vinci

It is something I completely believe in at my own level of life. I never felt bored in learning things I loved, from knowing about films, knowing a few topics about computers, directors and film making, books of criminals like Dial D for Don, Dongri to Dubai, Black Friday, random fantasy stories, etc.., topics.

I read various works by philosophers, authors, film directors, and others during the covid lockdown, which lasted almost a year, and I never got tired of it even though it once took me 10 hours straight in a day.

Podcasts containing my audio recordings, I spoke haphazardly, short stories I created with random thoughts, knowing about writing methods, learning more about podcasts, knowing how to write blogs, and rarely caring about my academics.

During my graduation, I noticed one of my friends, Akshay, doing a lot of study and research on his favourite subject or topic, spending hours in the library and never getting tired of the task. Rather from feeling unhappy or fatigued, his interest and curiosity encouraged him to learn new things and keep active.

I am certain type of guy who is obviously interested in learning about issues about which I'm enthusiastic about, I will never stopped studying and learning about things I'm inerested in, and I always willed to find a way to grow in order to get the most out of my available resources.

Even when the odds are stacked against me, it is my passion that drives me forward in learning, I moment I figured out how to learn is the minute I learned how to figure.

CHAPTER THREE

Rules, I never followed...

In technical words, rules are developed to state or make us follow particular policies on how to live, such as the dress code to follow, the speed limit to obey when driving—which govern practically every human interaction. So it's the rules that were desgnied for social purpose and societal surviavl, from school uniform dress code to government's law for certain things to live.

It was then back ages, The Hammurabi code of laws, a collection of 282 rules, established standards for commercial interactions and set fines and punishments to meet the requirements of justice, Hammurabi's Code was carved onto a massive, finger-shaped black stone stele (pillar) that was looted by invaders and finally rediscovered in 1901.

You can actually get through the rules by browsing about them in the internet, they are actually interesting.

In fact, I never committed to the notion of rules.

The reason for this is that regulations, in my opinion, turn bright people become idiots since they are designed by fools in the majority of circumstances. Rules limit your thinking potential rather than encouraging you to go beyond your thoughts.

If a strong person is performing fantastic thinking, wait till you see what a weak person is capable of thinking.

Intelligent people did not build rules because they understood that people and their thoughts cannot be limited by rules; it is never your thoughts that you can limit to think in limits, it can be the rules of not driving beyond a certain speed limit, but it is the speed that exists beyond the rules where you can actually learn.

As a result, because regulations impact your views, I consider them a waste of time in a social environment. I've never genuinely followed rules in my life; perhaps I was made to obey, but it's in my nature to appear to.

The only regulation I recall following in school and college was to wear a uniform. I never believed in the uniform method or process because the people who designed it or applied it to their institutions believed that by following the uniform dress code rule, people would actually consider everyone to be equal and that we needed to live together, but instead it's where they pretend to live and survive together.

If rules are meant to be created to certainly make someone, a group or a mob controlled in an order to exist I belive it's certainly their own aspect of maintaning a term called discipline or something, but it does make an indvidual to think less and at times makes the thinking capability to zero.

If it can be a rule regarding a college environment like college hours where one need to attend college exactly at 8AM in the morning and need to leave at some other time, I believe it's the timetable consideration make a student miserable.

Most of the rules are meant to make someone miserable, it's never even nature that created or meant the creatures to follow rules but it's the animals and we pretending apart from them creating and desgning our own rules in terms of unnatural ones and believe rules make the life of one who follow them to be the happiest and beautiful ones, Nature being the supreme let everyone left in freedom so as then it ensures freedom of learning things and making progress out of things.

CHAPTER FOUR

Traveling and Exploring

"How can you wonder your travels do you no good, when you carry yourself around with you?"

Socrates

I used to travel a lot when I was younger and I adore travelling and seeing new locations. My mother and her colleagues used to organise a lot of excursions all around India.

I used to get so thrilled for the vacations and wait for the time when we boarded our train to the location or city we were going to see whenever they fixed up one place or city to visit and planned certain things for travelling a month in advance.

It used to be those days when I was experiencing the life of train rides, and most of the time in my voyage plan, that travelling period played the greatest and longest function. I traveled to cities like Delhi, Agra, Mumbai, Chennai, Munnar(KERALA) and visited places like AIIMS, Bombay IIT (currently called Mumbai), tea estates of Kerala, Spice garden of Munnar, Varanasi and etc..,

Every visit, every excursion, and every adventure I do is remembered in my heart rather than my head. It was then that I met a few folks who helped to make my voyage beautiful, fun, and unforgettable. Because the majority of my travelling is done with my mother's coworkers, it was their children that I used to meet and become friends with, and we used to have a good time together.

During my time in Delhi, I met the daughter of one of my mother's coworkers, who was pursuing a bachelor's degree at the time I was in sixth grade, and she was the one who taught me a lot about a few tips and tricks, travel, and tech phrases that I'm interested in.

We used to wander the streets of Delhi, picking up unusual outfits, trinkets, food, and beverages. We used to listen to music, take odd photos, and do a variety of other things, It was that my conscious journey that I ever had in and then ages later I met another person where he did his part in my journeys.

On may 12th, 2018 it was then I met a person named Kausik where in a fraction of seconds we behaved to be friends from ages. It was then the period I enjoyed and it was him who made my journey special and memorable. All my past experiences of random journeys and my tours around cities and places gave me unforgettable memories to remember.

The people I met made my journeys special, the books that enlightened me about traveling, the habits, discipline, hobbies I created and developed myself during these journeys. It's the exploring I enjoyed more than the term traveling. It used to be me and Kausik exploring Varanasi, having a random clicks, roaming in the streets and ghats of Varanasi. We used to discuss and talk a lot about many contexts and concepts of exploring. We used to explore places of Kashi aka Varanasi, temples, spots that are attractive, food etc.

I believe Exploring is something interesting rather than the term traveling. The reason is that, I consider exploring is something you go unplanned whereas Traveling is something you plan to do or visit.

During my journeys to cities and places, I was habituated to explore them. It's the history I got from people over there, food I enquire about, places to visit near my stay, culture I respect, tradition I love, dance I try to perform, music I hear, clothing I try and many more.

When I went to Delhi and Bombay (AKA Mumbai), I went to the IITs. The world of IIT occupied my thoughts for several days. The desire to study at IIT is a fleeting concept in my mind that gradually removed by the reason of hating math.

The tea estates of Munnar, Frozen cold of Ganga river in Haridwar, Ghats of Varanasi, Streets of Bombay, Dynasties of Delhi, Beaches, Boat rides, Hyderabad's Charminar, Temples of Tamilnadu, Pamban bridge of Rameswaram, Sunrise and sunset of Kanyakumari, moments of Monuments and many places and the names they are given or considered.

I learnt a lot from the places I visited, I stayed, I clicked in my camera, the people I visited along with made my days memorable that are worth memorizing lot number of times a day.

One who finds himself traveling, helps himself in self-discovery. It is the self-examination which arises while traveling and discovering. So it was then I began speaking Hindi in Delhi for myself on random occasions such as ordering food, knowing information, questioning about the destination I needed to reach, and many more.

Speaking Hindi was something that startled me about the aspect of "I know HINDI" to the second of me. I had never learned Hindi before, and it was then that I discovered something about myself: I knew Hindi by chance, and that was what helped me learn more about myself.

While travelling throughout the world, one discovers unexpected characteristics about himself, such as his thoughts, the decisions he makes, and the care he receives, among other things.

I certainly believe one must travel around the globe once a year. It does help him explore the places he visits, introducing himself to the world, people he makes as friends on the way to reaching his destination and maybe meeting someone with the same destination which he may or can walk together later on.

It's the mechanical world that you and me hate and curse every night, plan a journey the very next second, switch off your phone for few days, go on a travel and explore yourself. I firmly think that there will come a day in my calendar when I will leave my house with no baggage and nothing, begin travelling the globe, and never return.

CHAPTER FIVE

Money: Value and Worth

"The only question with wealth is, what do you do with it?"

- John D. Rockefeller

In my opinion, money is something I have never cared about or considered. It's never something like, I mean, useless or inept, but it's something like, I didn't care about saving, fear of losing it, and worrying about my expenditure and stuff.

When my father handed me an amount of Rs.500 for my birthday, I used to blow it on a movie, trying new foods, and going to a random location, then to return home with 10 or 20 change.

So here's the point: I think of money as POWER rather than paper, and sure, the piece of paper did have power here, and I like to use the term POWER wherever feasible, which I do frequently in my situation in any context.

People originally used money as a response to the inquiry or exchange of "What's in return?"

In technical terms, it may be a person out in the wild or jungle in the era of stone or rock, or whatever, who had the notion of clearing the mess of grass, trees, and rocks to free up space for something called a HOUSE, also known as shelter.

So, in order to make his idea a reality, he needed men to work for him, and as they needed to work for you, you needed to pay or trade back or in return, which can be stated as if you do something in return for what someone else has done for you, you do it because they did that thing for you, and this eventually created a path for barter system, which ultimately led to the term money being coined.

Here, the value of the job they have done for you is determined by the people with whom you must work, and the potentiality of money is demonstrated by spending rather than earning and saving.

"To create MONEY, you must spend MONEY" - PLAUTUS

So if your goal is to make money out of your money you must spend the money to make progress of making money and the money you spend needs disclipline and plan which depends on your expenditure of money.

When I see or hear someone remark, "MONEY transforms people," I prefer to listen at first and then pretend to hear it. Money just meets your needs, wants, and desires based on your choice and categorization, and I think that no third party or third person can govern one's ideas and emotions unless they are formed within.

It is the virus within the body that creates or learns the way for foreign viruses to enter. If one doesn't have the desire in his deepest dark side I believe none and no-one can help him to get thim into brain from external source.

Even if there are quotes saying " EMOTIONS AND DESIRES ARE MEANT TO BE CONTROLLED" I belive these kind of quotes are useful in books of "Cursive writing" for kids of grade 2, so it's useless to believe you can control one's emotions and things with quotes.

So money plays an important role in our daily lives; it is the prize we are supposed to give to someone for their job, skill, art, technical expertise, and so on and with considerations, you got the price settings, which and where every product started to have an average price, and it does have a difference between the price of a work or an art form with me and the price of a Picasso, because of the knowledge he has, master he is, expert in his work or skill or art whatever the term is, and it does change because of the worth of the art.

It can be me writing this book with minimal knowledge and it can be someone else out there who are called as Masters and Experts having a vast knowledge about their skill, art and in being master in any of the field they love to know about and work on.

So, indeed, the worth here depends with the difference of value and worth.

Here, Value can be termed or tagged as something called as important, majority cases it's consider to be in figurative terms and Worth can be termed as something you tag for what they deserve to.

It can be the value, usually termed as the price you regulate for you work and worth is something you deserve to be entitled to.

Money has never been my objective; rather, it has aided me in establishing a route toward attaining things that I am passionate about, it's just a way that helped me in knwoing terms of what all can I do with a little amount in my hand.

So, rather than earning money I say spend it, it's then I believe the potentiality can be proved rather than storing or saving it.

CHAPTER SIX

Book, An art of expression

"A reader does live a thousand lives before he dies."

It was then in 2016, when I visited Mumbai, when I stayed at a home of knowns, and it was there that I met two youngsters, one of which, the elder one, introduced me to books. The "Amar chitra katha" novels and a few fiction volumes piqued my interest. It was her interpretation of the literature she read, the hidden meaning she gleaned from the texts, that took me aback. She liked to brag about her extensive book collection. Her father used to bring her books whenever he travelled to different countries for important meetings and related events. She used to have a collection of 300 books of "Amar Chitra Katha" comics.

"Into the Storm," about a girl and her friend attempting to get their father to the beach from a large toranodo, was the first book I ever read in my school library, that I finished in 2-3 days., and I adored the characters. It was then that I began to read books of many genres and types. The books of Desmond Bagely, H.G. Wells Invisible man and few more books were those I read in intial days. It was then with the help of internet I used to know about various authors and used to read thier books. The books of Film directors like **Steven Speilberg, Quentin Tarantino, Alfred Hitchcock** and etc helped me diversed my knowledge from book to book and refering it with film to film.

It may be a moon passing over our heads in the night, but it is the author who can communicate his thoughts on a moon in a more intriguing and unusual way than the casual and customary view we have as regular people. They tend to bring out the maximum possible good ones from the odinary ones which are actually extraodinary, the moon over our heads can be something the usual ones we observe daily and again it be the same us feeling and observing it on a random occasion and feel like It's beautiful, in the same way the writers, authors are someone that loved to praise the beautful factors of the moon we rarely observe.

"There is so much to read that one life isn't enough" from Cousins, 1959.

Whenever I read a random book, it is something I get to know something new. It can be about a thought, an idea, perspectives, knowledge from one's experience and many things. In my school, one of my teachers, Srikanth sir, addressed the history about BOOKs, he disclosed about the history of books from it's first origin to the book present in his hand. He explained in such way that, It then prompted me to consider **WHY SOMETHING LIKE A BOOK?**

I used to think, why did people invented or created something like a book and eventually found vast reasons and answers where few of them were, to write about the history, to share one's thoughts, ideas, opinions, views etc, and there raised a question from somewhere around from my brain asking,

Why to write something in form of book?

Isn't it something that people can make sure of rememberance of the event and pass it to generations orally than something like a medium of books?

With the passage of time, I figured out an answer stating that it can be the origin of the story with 100 words, and when it comes to disclosing it to others, it can be the 90 words carried forward, and finally it can be the 50 words. Here, it's never about the human brain's inability to remember things, but rather it's about remembering things we loved, we were interested in, and I only remember a maximum of 50 words answers for a 250 word essay question that I'm supposed to write. So it's the book here been an alternative for storage of information and preparing a book with something called as requirements which make a book to have a long life and easy to store anywhere.

The old books does have an aura in itself which can be experienced by few, the thoughts in it are something far better than the thoughts of present days, the moment we read the old books, it's then we are meant to be in an environment where we are gonna meet the finest people of the society.

CHAPTER SEVEN

Nature I escape to

"As in everything, nature is the best instructor"

- Adolf Hitler

The ultimate almighty power with the ability to create heaven and hell on Earth. Nature has always been with us and for us.

The birth of nature is something that has many theoretical conceptions of all sorts, but it is still alright, it may be any cause that helped to develop a word nature and it is the nature from which we are made.

I enjoy exploring woods with many plant species, cliffs, valleys, mountains, beaches, oceans, and other sites in the collection known as nature.

Indeed, it's from where we actually came up and it's where we stay in after clearning place fo us.

It was then, in 2019, that I visited Kerala for the first time, and it was a place called Munnar that drew my entire attention to it; I adored the place so much that I was in a trance of Munnar even after leaving and returning from it; it's a resemblance of natural beauty; I adored the gardens, tea estates, mountains, sunrises, and rains; There's one thing I really liked about it: I didn't see a single fan in any of the houses, and the water supply they have is far better to the rest of the world: it's subsurface water, which the inhabitants accept as a gift from God and drink without boiling or treating.

The Spice Garden, Munnar does have a numerous collection of plats, spices, few animals like rabbits, ducks and few more and the location behind the location with a river flowing in beneath the roof of tree branches is something like a feast for my eyes.

Nature is something superior to us and it's always been the more we think we need it is the more it, it's the nature taught us, thought for us meanwhile it's us that thought our ownself than thinking about the ones that went thinking for us.

CHAPTER EIGHT

Why are criminals so popular?

Being against evil doesn't make you good.

-Ernest Hemingway

Crimes, in my opinion, are one of the society's sustaining foundations. It is for this reason that I feel the laws we have evolved, as well as society advancements in terms of legal aspects, are constructed with a crime in mind.

Criminals are defined as those who have violated or failed to observe the laws and regulations established by a country and by a few individuals in response to a few things or situations. Since the first ever heard crime, I've been curious in the criminal's mental states during the time of the offence, the reasons, the cause, and many other variables that led to the commission of the crime.

It's never about the question of "Who they are?" but the reason for "Why?". I feel that the 'WH' question style is the most effective way for us to learn about anything. Any query of WHY, I think, prompts a follow-up question of WHAT, piques your interest in HOW, prompts you to inquire about WHO, and eventually allows you to choose WHICH.

The research of the reason for a crime actually defines it rather than just tagging it with some random name. For example, theft for the absence of lacking is something that leads to committing a theft activity, while murder under considerations of anger, conflict, and fear can be reason to commit a murder crime.

So, I believe it's the phrase for evaluating the circumstances that actually led to the commission of a certain crime, it's the cause to be known to prevent a crime rather than penalising it with no results, if it's the dread you believe exists, it's the fear they pretend exists.

The will of a criminal is so powerful that when he actually aim to rule a business, he does develop a empire based on his crime activities.

His thoughts can be so immensly powerful while considering thoughts of anyone else. He can build an empire out of dust, and all he needs is the determination to do so. Crimianls all around the globe operate their businesses from all around the world.

He can be anyone from any country controlling their men staying anywhere with just a 30 seconds phone call. It's never about considering them to be the good side or to the evil side of the society but it depends with perspectives and opinions. It can be a tiger hunting down a deer for it's hungry cubs resulting to be a good father but whereas remain to be hated by fawns. So it's view of us in considering what's a crime and whats's not a crime.

So, what was the very first crime?

What is the rationale for this?

What elements enabled it to conduct a crime?

The hunger, very first reason for a crime to commit.

It can be some random kid on streets attempting a random theft and with the earned money he did went to a hotel and had some food of his own like. As there exist a random quote, "Hunger is the reason for attempt of a crime", here the desire to satisfy the hunger is the reason for crime

It can be an animal in nature at a point of time in million years ago went under consideration of unavailability of the usual leafy food and went under a food of flesh of other animals, here the exact reason may vary but one of the reasons can be the nature of considering the food they prefer to eat, to eat the weak one by a strong one, it can be a fly eating a random available food and it can be a frog eating the fly and it can be a snake eating a frog and it can be an Eagle eating that snake, so the ultimate powerful one ever exist with death of weaker ones and that's the nature.

The reason of them being popular is something I ever think of, what actually made them popular or interested by the people....?

When I was at age of around 8 years it was then I ever heard of death of Osama bin laden, I used to witness a lot of documentaries, reports on him and etc activities performed by media and government agencies and my first ever experience and after started to read news paper articles about crimes it helped me to read about what all happened or the cause of death, who was been killed by whom is something written in papers and discussed among people and it was then when a question raised in my inner self stating that the, knowing who is the victim and accused and the cause of death is something fine but still the reason of why is something always stays unknown to the world.

I believe it's that termed, called and known as reason to commit a crime is something that is meant to be studied and analyzed and it actually help in a easier way to slove out more issues where when have the common base of reason in terms of commiting a crime.

CHAPTER NINE

Alone or Lonely...?

Alternative HEAVEN environmental setup on the Earth

It is the peace you build with yourself that matters, not the peace you make with others. Rather than being socialist, I used to schedule time for myself to read books, watch movies, and search the internet for weird and fascinating information. You lose yourself when you stay in a crowd.

In my my level, I always loved aloness and I never ever left loneliness which is caused by absence of 2nd person, the reason is that I always loved my ownself rather than liking the second person's presence, the reason is that I do say to people in terms of saying it doesn't matter your absence to me which may sound as demeaning their presence but still it's my honest to speak out and it's always their choice in making decision to travelling along with me or taking a turn. Even while staying among hundreds, I can still be alone and enjoy.

I feel that everyone who remains awake adoring one's presence is actually loathing one's own presence and oneself, when you feel comfortable in presence of second person it does sound as escaping from your ownself, if it's our own presence being boring to you, how can you atleast pretend it's something liked by people around you?

Those that stay in the crowd lose their uniqueness, and all of their rational thoughts are covered with junk covers, while insane notions throw reasoning out the window and take control of the region. Spend some time alone and you'll learn a lot. It is the period when one want to spend time with oneself. Knowing yourself is the most powerful weapon you can have ever.

Self-discovery is essential for understanding oneself.

Alone is not the same as loliness; aloness is something you want to be apart from the world, but loliness is something you feel the world has abandoned you.

The phrase "lonliness" and "loneliness" were first used in literature in the 17th century. Naturalist John Ray published a lexicon of uncommon terms in 1674. In his list, he listed "loneliness," which he defined as a phrase used to characterise areas and individuals "far from neighbours", Solving loneliness was simple in the 17th century, when it was mainly confined to the countryside. It only took a return to society.

Loneliness, on the other hand, has subsequently gone within — and has become much more difficult to treat. It can't always be fixed by company since it's taken up home within thoughts, even those of individuals living in lively cities. Loneliness in the modern day involves more than just being physically separated from other people. Instead, it's an emotional condition in which you feel apart from others — even if you aren't.

Someone who is surrounded by others, or even accompanied by friends or a partner, might experience loneliness. The wildness has now taken up residence within us. One of the reasons loneliness is regarded as so dangerous now is that there is no obvious therapy for it: the abstraction is terrible.

Surprisingly, the secret to overcoming modern loneliness may not be to try to make it go away, but to find ways to dwell within its abstractions, talk through its contradictions, and seek out people who feel the same way.

I've never felt lonely because I've never placed any value on the existence of a second person; however, the majority of people do feel lonely because they place value on the existence of someone else, and when that person is no longer present, you find a way to feel lonely, whereas Aloness is something where you value yourself, your own company, and you make time to be with you, for you, and by you.

It can never be you listening a class with mob around you where you are actually tended to learn it alone, we are programmed to learn it alone but I believe it's something that we are meant to learn it actually apart anf away from mob where you do develop yourself and you create yourself and when you stay in the crowd it's something you stay and remain in the crowd forever.

The brains out there are filled with dead thoughts, desires, ideas and they are someone considered to be the ZOMBIE. So ZOMBIES are something that stay up in the crowd and the survivals stay away from the ZOMBIES and stay alone for survival.

CHAPTER TEN

Memento Mori that inspired me

Memento mori, it's a Latin phrase which actually mean, "remember you must die", It's the ancient romans who developed the concept of Memento mori. It does consists of square boxes on a total count of 80 rows and 52 columns which represent a lifespan of 80 years. Every box you tick as complete is every week ran out of your life.

The first known use of memento mori was in 1598, The statement is thought to have originated in ancient Rome, where slaves following generals on victory parades muttered the words as a reminder of their commander's mortality in order to keep them from succumbing to hubris (excessive pride and self-confidence). From the mediaeval period to the present, the notion has become a common cliché in the visual arts.

It was during the time of lockdown, where when I was randomly searching something interesting to read about and finally poped up with a result of MEMENTO MORI.

When I first learned about this concept, being conscious of your mortality may seem frightening, yet it is a powerful stimulus for introspection and transformation.

It puts everything in perspective, melts away concerns, and clears the way for you to focus on what actually matters.

The weekly practise of filling in a new square will bring you into the present now, enhance your perspective on life, and provide you with the inspiration and drive to act quickly week after week.

Everyone among us want to do something interesting that makes us excited or passionate to do, for example, flying high above the clouds, skydives, scuba dives beneath the seas, unplanned journey to do, staring up a business, a coffee shop, a restruant, a company maybe, but since most of us are afraid of results, the process, the starting troubles in us make us feel "maybe next time" and we eventually postpone it to later where we miss the chance of doing it and we end up in regret, it's the motivation or lack of remebering the term we are gonna die.

It was back then, when I decided to do some random work or study that I had planned but put off until later, that I learned about Memento mori and its phrase, Remember you must die, and the calendar I read about, and each week when I tick a square box, I remind myself that I'm getting close to death.

Death, in my opinion, is not dreadful or frightening, but it is a scenario in which you can't do anything and that scared me the most.

"The classical man's worst fear was inglorious death; the modern man's worst fear is just death"

-Nassim Nicholas Taleb

I was always frietenged death which make me to do nothing else, Imagine waking up to a pleasant morning, and after experiencing the comfort for a while, you began to realise you are unable to move, and after a while, you started to notice people out there are weeping, their eyes filled with tears, and you continue to experience the existence while the remaining are sad for your absence you can't move, talk, or act in any of their forms to make a note of or call their attention, and finally you lose the shape of life, and beyond the wall of death is always something unknown to us, which is what makes us fearful and in my context I'm afraid of not being able to do anything I wished for is something I'm afraid of than the DEATH which is something beyond and larger than our ratio of imagination.

So it was then that I began to list and figure out what I was frightened of, what I intended to do, what I wished to accomplish, and a few other things, and I began to work on them. It may be an impromptu excursion that I take on the spur of the moment to travel around cities and see things that are on my TO DO LIST.

This book is something I thought to write and started to know about the technical terms for writing a book and started with the help of my knowledge I collected or gained from experiences of my past, films, books and my friends that eventually helped me in learning about things.

I believe every indivudal should take a print out of a Memento mori calender, mark his birthday and eventually with due time tick the square box everytime a week complete he get's into an awareness of weeks or time wasted by him and start to work on things he wished to do whatever he is passionate about and help in focusing things which truly matter.

CHAPTER ELEVEN

Quotes that inspired me....

Quotations ae something that are phrased out in a sentence which can even have hidden meaning built with known words, when you started to love a quote it's actually the reason that, even that quote is hidden in you but in state of jumbledness, when a writer puts words that stay jumbled in brain and make sentence out of it, it is does then we feel like, it's something relevant to our thoughts.

At times, it's not possible to explain an answer in format of sentences built with hundreds of words and it can be time waste and useless in explaining your whole term of idealogy and eventually end up in terming and framing it in form of a quote.

In considering the same way, it's few quotes that inspired me a lot. They are;

- "Life is not a problem to be solved, but a reality to be experienced", Soren kierkegaard.
- "Facts do not cease to exist because they are ignored", Aldous Huxley.
- " The lonely one offers his hand too quickly to whomever he encounters", Friedrich Nietzsche.
- "The heaviest penalty for declining to rule is to be rules by someone inferior to yourself", Plato.
- "It's not supposed to be easy. Anyone who finds it easy is stupid", Charlie Munger.
- "I was in darkness, but it took three steps and found myself in paradise. The first step was a good thought, the second, a good

word; and the third, a good deed", Friedrich Nietzsche.

- " The difficulty comes from our lack of confidence", Seneca.
- "Difficulty is what wakes up the genius", Nassim Taleb.
- "In any given moment we have two options: to step forward into growth or to step back into safety.", Abraham maslow.
- "He will win who knows when to fight and when not to", Sun Tzu.
- "Any ideas, plan, or a purpose maybe replaced in the mind through repetition of thought", Napoleon Hill.
- "If you win, you need not have to explain....If you loose, you should not be there to explain", Adolf Hitler.
- "Anyone can deal with victory. Only the mighty can bear defeat", Adolf Hitler.
- "I swear by my life and my love of it that I will never live for the sake of another man, nor ask another man to live for mine.", Atlas Shrugged.
- "If you wanna be happy, be"
- "Compare yourself to who you were yesterday, not to who someone else is today", Jordan Peterson.

CHAPTER TWELVE

Think Different and consider alternatives

It is possible that we will spend some of our lives bored. Boredom may be caused by a number of factors, one of which is ROUTINE. During the lockdown, it was I who decided to try something new and finally launched a blog using Blogger and podcasts with the Anchor app and published few blogs, podcasts, read books relating to filmology, books of directors and many things.

Never ever opt to do things in routine formats.

- Instead of taking the same route to college every day, take a detour and see a movie at a neighbouring theatre.
- It doesn't have to be the same clothes you wear every day; instead, try something fresh.
- Instead than listening to the same local music, consider listening to music from a different nation.
- It may be the same language you speak every day, or it could be a new one that you learn and make mistakes in while speaking.
- Every weekend, try a new place to visit and return by learning and experiencing new things.,
- Once a week or once a month, try a different food kind and get a fresh taste.
- Watch a random film of no language barrier and expeience a new cinema than the usual ones you watch,

- Try out new hair styles, try specs, talk to new people, read something new.

These I believe on an average of doing something new and maybe there exist a lot more things to try out, these are something I marked to do or to try out one day....

Change your lifestyle once a month to experiece something new, it can be choosing outfits of early 20's, music of 90's, movie of random genres you never experienced, it's our brain that need refreshment from the same old things, so it's the alternative you need to consider from the old and boring concepts, there's always fun in considering the alternatives apart from the old things we learn, it can be the same old math tricks used by you to solve problems but there do exist an alternative way to solve out the problem in most easy and effective way, but still we are intended to learn the same old one..........

- It's normal to react in predictable ways to predictable events.
- It's normal to have an uncommon reaction to an unexpected scenario.
- It's normal to react in predictable ways in unexpected situations.
- It's odd to react unusually to an ordinary issue.

I really feel that being bored and routine with oneself is something that will eventually kill you.

CHAPTER THIRTEEN

My views on the Internet

In technical words, the internet is a method of linking individuals through a particular medium through which one may access anything he wants and communicate whatever he wants using numerous channels contained within the medium.

It was during my second grade summer, and as I was ready to attend third grade, my father gave me a laptop, which was unusual and out of the ordinary for me. It featured a tiny display, unlike the typical PC system has its own monitor that looks like a mini tv, it had a keyboard attached rather than a separate keyboard arrangement connected to the PC through a USB connection, and a few more aspects sparked my curiosity.

It was my friend, Sarath, who ever introduced to the computer present in his house, he used to help me in exploring and experiencing the computer, about it's working and the parts that helped the system to work for a specific task instructed and in time being my father gifted me and my brother a laptop and it was something new apart from the computers I ever experienced and explored, it doesn't have the CPU case as of the usual PC setup and the speakers being in-built, thin display, keybord attached, closing lid and few things were actually something that made me feel curious in knowing about the laptop I was gifted with and eventually my father ever got our first internet connection termed usually as Wi-fi, it was then my first ever introduction was to the google and youtube, while searching a random place it's the videos that were suggested by the google and got to know about the youtube.

After in time being along with internet, I believe Internet is something termed to be it's own kind of world, where we are the species living in it with an internet identity, the origin of purpose of internet is something related to communicate and share data between each other, so it's the origin with 2 purposes and after around 50 years, we are here with a vast availability of purposes, options, choices, chances with enoromous availability of requirements and access availability.

In my terms, I believe internet has something become an habit for kids of kinder-garden to the adults in garden. They go through options of opening the application, clicking on search, clicking about something they want about and then they have the opted results they searched for and select among them, in kids it can be the cartoons, songs they love, animated shows and meanwhile in adults, it can be the films they are intrested to watch, people collecting information regarding thier study, work, research etc.,

So, here the internet has helped so well resuleting in geting things of whatever we wished for, it can be something where when we don't know the name of something, it can be an red colour fruit, a creature of randomly you found in your garden, a type of flower you found interesting in a park, food, locations to visit when visted a random city, to know the directions, to plan for a journey in advance, knowing about someone's details with the help of their number even, so it's the internet that helpped to make something beyond our imagination and in considering and admitting the fact about internet that states, internet is created by humans themselves, so here, human brain is powerful than internet, I agree in considering the fact of human brain is something that actually helped in making something powerful called as internet and it's the ultimate reason that helped me in learning vast things and assisted me in writing this book.

CHAPTER FOURTEEN

Character, I don't have

Knowing you don't have a character is a sign of wisdom.

People pretend to have character. It's always something I think people think they have.

Intelligent individuals do not believe in character terms. It is never the case that we belong to a certain category of behaviour. It's possible that we're different in some ways from folks we despise and in others from those we adore. So, when it comes to our own amount of freedom, our behaviour varies depending on who we are with.

As of the same case, majority of the people actually does have a character, they pretend to it but it's something even majority of the people don't know that it doesn't exist.In layman's words, I feel that character refers to all of the traits that a person has acquired.

My reason for a character doesn't exist is that, while in a process of getting matured, acquiring knowledge, achieving goals, can be short or long, in process of progess we does learn a lot and acquire things to our brain and at times the opinions and thoughts does change with time to time about concern things, it can be our character thinking positivly but at times we may have to think in negative factors that actually false out our character.

It can be you thinking while doing a chapter of math in way resulting considering math is an easy subject but the same you can hate it while solving out much difficult problems. We maybe back to our thoughts once things get better but still character is defined out there as terms fixed, but in my opinion it should be something a lot flexible.

For me, character is something I pretended to have, I always warned people around me not to have any intended opinion or option in believing me, trusting me because it something I never manage to stand on.

If I learn anything today, I manage to adapt it to myself, and the following day, I learn something new. It may be being terrible on a day after reading or viewing crime-related material such as movies, reports, books, or articles, or with a source of something and It can be the same me being good the next day with a few acts of helping people, respect, and something else with a filled stuff from books again, articles about random help, and so on, so it's the same thing that inspired or liked by me one day and something liked the next day, and it happens in the majority of cases, and it's never about something I pretend to support my statement but the reality is something I considered into existence to let the blind have a look at.

"Doesn't that make yourself degrading to be different every day, changing with each thinking, and for not being the same way you were yesterday and not keeping your word?" was one of the questions posed by one of my Diploma classmates.

I said that, the problem for being trustworthy is that you need to stay everytime the same and you can never experience new things, if it's something you are meant to attend college everyday and being honest to attend daily and maintaining the attedance, you can't even know something new. It just make your days filled with boredom. The moment I don't be honest or trustworthy I loose people and indeed it can be termed as loosing the weight which is actually good for health.

CHAPTER FIFTEEN

Attention: Music

"Music is life itself"

- Louis Armstrong

The burble caused by waterfalls, the sound of water dipping on rocks, the rustling of leaves, cricket noises, owl hootings at night, birds chirping in the mornings, and other natural sounds are thought to be the first step for music ever made. It was at this point that the man began to consider music.

Music is something that carries hundreds of feelings with it. It might be the lively mornings of birds, owls hooting about the late evenings, lion roars for communication, dolphin whistles, and so on. It was in class seven that I first learned about sound, music, and noise. Simply put, sound is produced by a pattern of vibrarions.

Music is anything formed with a tune of music, which is created with a suitable sequence of sounds that makes hearing the music pleasurable and makes the experience out to be beautiful. Noise is simply defined as something that is unpleasant to hear. Music has a long history that predates humanity.

There can be many technicals for consideration of music but in simple, when I first considered "what to listen?" it was the pleasant music I started to enjoy. Songs can be defined as something composed with music and stuff called lyrics and with an art of singing. It's the music that I love to hear whenever I get tired, felt bored or whenever I'm free.

The music does contain a very strong emotion if understood you get into a state of mind where you never wanna come back out from the world of music. Instrumental music is something I max prefer to listen. While considering the songs, the lyrics, the music, the sounds, the dips and peeks and if any other technicals in considertion, I believe it's the trance we exist whenever we love a certain song.

It can be a song of "BABY" from Justin beaber many teens once practised, "See you again" where many felt for and many other more and considering one of my fav music directors known Ilayaraja, where I listen any of his songs once or twice a day and at times I sing the lyrics with reference to voice of singer and practise songs whenever I'm free and alone and with time and situation you exist-in, as said, it's the music that hold an emtion so hard, when put into an act, it can make us think, feel and cry too.

There is no greater language to speak and convey than music.

CHAPTER SIXTEEN

What if one day....?

Imagine waking up to the sound of birds chirping on your window grills, and you began to search for family but found none, searched every room but none, and began to believe "maybe went out."

After a while of freshening up, you called out to your parents and discovered their phones were in your house itself, and you began to feel tense and thought of making yourself to relax, when you switched on your television, all of the stations went dark with some blurry sounds and visuals, so you went upstairs to your balcony and noticed no one on the streets and no noise from people.

You began calling your friends but no one answered, you shut your door and walked out into the streets but found no one, you travelled and roamed and roamed on roads but no one was located, and you gradually began to understand that YOU ARE NOW ALONE....!,

This feeling of being alone may initially cause you to be happy because you can drive cars of your choice, eat food of your choice, stay in luxury rooms, have showers, bathtubs, swimming pools, watch a movie in a theatre, petting a dog, cat, and possibly radom of your own kind, days of no rules and no regulations, and so on.

Apart than getting high results in school or whatever else, I pray once a month for this dream to come true. You will see none and no one will ever see you again, and you will be the last person ever remaining in humanity. It's also something I envisage with a morning and a view of high tides and tsunami waves, meteor assaults, volcanic eruptions, nuclear weapons activation, and finally realising it's apocalypse.

To concede the reality, Zombies are something me and my sibling fantasize about in end times perspective. As of motion pictures like Zombieland, World War Z, and Train to Busan, we generally used to talk about our jobs. If there should arise an occurrence of our insane dream working out as expected, we used to examine our jobs, where we participate together in the working of dividers around our picked house, and wall over them with an electrical association with them, planning a home out of transport, weapons like automatic rifles connected to the back of it, stuff like iron spikes in front of the vehicle.

I certainly believe that there exist a day where our fantasies, thoughts, dreams does come true but at the same time it does sound crazy while appearing from terrific to terrible.

I'm waiting for day where maybe, I read newspaper with which a headline of Deadline, and certainly wanna sit on top of a skyscapper or on mountain with a view where I can watch people fighting and killing each other and then BOOM......... with just fraction of seconds everything goes white with shock waves an dust waving so fastly while I start to eat out my cheese burger I made and as of the popular web-series STRANGER THINGS, I wished a lot of times for similar supernatural or unique powers and being out as a freak among the commons.

Having a ghost as a friend, someone from the future who can assist me in travelling through time, knowing things, and many other things are things I fantasised about and used to imagine.

To maintain the same feeling for a while, I used to watch films in the genre of fantasy and movies in the related genre of super hero films or a story plot where a super hero is a friend to the lead character, where the character here is a kid or a teenager, and I used to imagine my ownself and feel a high for a while.

CHAPTER SEVENTEEN

Logics and Emotions

When you are dealing with a person,

remeber you are dealing with a person of emotions

Logics are what I believe to be a proper or fair method to studying anything, in which you evaluate the facts and factors rather than taking it as it is or thinking it to be nothing.

Emotions, on the other hand, are supposed to be those unreasonable ideas and behaviours.

It was back then during the age of medieval period, a greek philosopher Parmenides invented logic while living on a rock in egypt. Instead of just offering a picture of reality, Parmenides was the first philosopher to utilise an extensive argument to support his beliefs. However, utilising arguments is not as the same as studying them, and parmendies never systematically defined or researched argumentation principles in and of themselves. Indeed, there is little indication that he was even aware of the implict inference rules employed in presenting his philosophy.

According to Karl Albrecht, sequential thinking is the foundation of all logical reasoning. This technique entails organising the key concepts, facts, and conclusions in an issue into a chain-like sequence that takes on significance in and of itself. Thinking rationally entails thinking in phrases.

Whereas, when considered the term Emotions, It's the book of Darwin's named Emotions in man and animals. In this book, Darwin attempted to expand his theory of natural selection beyond the evolution of physical structures and into the realm of mind and behaviour by investing how emotions may have developed as well.

In terms of considerations, all feeling follows the same pattern. When we consider an act or an event to a personal level or when we take things seriously, we intend to respond to them or act on them with the emotion of anger.

Anger is a powerful emotion that can change an act in an instant, limit our ideas or thinking capabilities, and make us inconceivable, leading us to do and take judgments that aren't always remedied or rectified, and cause us to experience regret for the rest of our lives. Any emotion that weakens a man is his adversary, and our focus on our feelings eventually weakens and renders us ineffectual.....

Emotions limit a man's ability to think; they don't make him evaluate or accept the realities around him, but rather make him feel that his ideas and considerations are more powerful than others', and they might lead him to regret or guilt.

Meanwhile, logics are something that help you a lot for survival. It tends to make you accept the things going around you than letting you to live out in an imagination of your own kind.....

It can be termed as the study of acts that go around us, it can be any individual with a tag of logical thinker where he/she analyze things around them and consider various feedbacks and come to a conclusion, it may or maynot be true or correct but still it helps in making progress from far better than emotions.

In my terms of experience, I felt things emotional in rare cases but still after a while it's the logic that helped me to understand myself in terms of thinking the possibilities of why and helped me to improve myself in aspect of constructing a defensive mechanism or defensive thought process from emotions that tend to control.

In conclusion, I'd like to explain that any emotion that weakens you is your adversary, and any reasoning that aids in thinking is your ally.

Love and Relationships

There's nothing here.......

Expert and Master

Michael jackson for Moon walk, Usama for Terriosts attack, USA for technologies, India for culture, Germany for it's engineering, China for it's manufacturing, Bangkok for it's tourism, Switzerland for it's majestic nature and many for many are meant to be a mark of their own nature. Here, Nature doesn't only sound about the trees, plants, animals, etc.., but also can be known as for it's inherent features, character, or qualities of something.

I believe expert is someting considered, in my level of understanding, to be the one known for his own kind and format of performing an act or activity, he does have a vast knowledge in his work and skillful towards his job. If you are so interested in learning about something, your ultimate goal is never to score 100's about the subject or skill you wanna learn, it's the knowledge you learn and put into action.

Expert are created when knowledge is put into action and remained to be the people having enough skiils in thier own level of work or performance in task.

It can be making a lemonade with average taste, taking more time in considering the required salt or sugar, water levels, lemon juice and things and it can be someone like a person who own a lemonade shop making it with a better taste than mine. So, the point is that an expert is something who have a lot of experience and the repeated action of the same task helped him to reach a point of good and then to the best taste.

Indeed, it can also be those factors of interest, passion and commitment does help in making things work from odinary to extraodinary.

All masters, in my opinion, are experts, and not all experts are masters. It does have various facts in consideration for a master as an expert and an expert not as a master.

It can be you knowing the skill of your particular task and performing it with failure at first, enough performance in the second and you better yourself everytime you practise it and evry time you practise it you reach a level of good, better, best and expert and,

Master here is something that is completely different, he does have complete knowledge about the subject or an art or about a technique, it can be a expert in karate or whatever art form performing the kick in an excellent but it's the master who do know here about when to perform the act of the KICK.

So, to master oneself, study while developing your expertise.

CHAPTER TWENTY

Struggles, Failure and Success

"To avoid an action that might have harmful consequences for us-that would mean a ban on decent actions in general."

- Friedrich Nietzsche

Reading the terms failure and struggle may make you feel uneasy, yet reading the word and term Success may make you feel at ease.

The reason behind this is because the words, "failure" and "struggle" make people feel humiliated or scared to look at or read about them. I believe the explanations are societal concepts that are fed into the brain and then seen as bad features.

When you make a certain decision, whether professional or personal, you make a decision based on the terms and circumstances that are available to you to consider, so when you make a decision of your own wish, you begin to work on it and eventually develop your idea and progressively attain a product out of your decision or from an idea.

While working on your concept, you develop a plan never to fail in the advancement of it, and when you believe in your choice, knowledge, and consideration of progress and strive towards it, you feel you will make a mark of success, but in due time or on numerous aspects, it may go wrong at times.

So I believe, **Failure is never discovered in the progress or process, but rather in the outcome.**

Why would I fail in math hundreds of times if failing is something I can anticipate or know ahead of time?

In society, success and failure are considered as reputational terms, with fools and idiots criticising you for your flaws and praising you for your accomplishments. I failed math multiple times in high school and college and never thought about it until my math instructor labelled me a failure, and the instant I disregarded it and him, I began to think beyond it.

Ignorance is one of the most effective defences against failure, yet failure, I believe, is a natural process of evolution that all species must go through. It's the tiger who has daily hunt failures and just once in ten hunts succeeds.

The drive to hunt and satisfy the tiger's hunger is a sensation that aids us in attaining everything we wish; it is the most powerful incentive a man can have in making things work for whatever he sets out to do.

So it's the perspective and comparision that defining your success, It might be the Titanic as proof for one of the terrible tragedies that occurred, or Harry Potter being a conventional hit for a wizard and magic based creative film, It can be considered that "2012" is a brand for disaster films, and then Avatar entered the ring and became a worldwide sensation for a science-fiction film, and eventually it can be considered that the films of now are the successful ones, and every film has its own type and format of success defined to it's own kind, and everytime you believe something is success, there's something that exists is beyond your imagination of success.

So success is, every place out there, labelled as the destination, but it's the journey that you finally make out of your works, if you make your work from an initial point of "strike of an idea" to eventually developing a plan, strategy in learning things relevant to your task. It can be this book represting my jouney in terms of defining and writing my thoughts, ideas and views which I wanna express and if I succeed in defining them in my own pensive way, it's the success I believe in my perspective.

Struggle is something I adore, and I've never understood the notion or meaning behind the phrase since once you start doing something you enjoy, you never want to stop. When you observe a kid on weekends, he love to play among the remaining of his age in a park where his/her mother struggle to take their child back to their bed.

It's never a kid who thinks about the injuries that has happened to him while playing his favourite sport and thinks of the next goal he need to make and later he gets himself a first-aid to clear them off. I feel it's something that has been unnaturally defined and established, it's never about the strggling period of an eagle in it's infant age learning to fly where as it's the same eagle start to fly after a period of 10 weeks, is it something that struggled to fly all these 10 weeks? It's the process it learnt of HOW? WHEN? WHAT? and WHERE? questions which does mean about, HOW to fly?, When to fly, WHAT are the requirements or techniques to fly? WHERE should I fly to?

Whenever I feel "Am I struggling ?" it's the thought I consider as a question that I do ask my ownself and in due time when sleeping I get an answer which do states that, it's the progress I'm making rather than taking it to hard.

But, in reality, it is the difficult times that drive you to study and know more than your ambitions, objectives, targets, and goals. It may be an eagle in its infancy attempting to soar, but it is the era of struggle that causes it to learn and know a lot, including where, when, and how.

So the difficult period you thought was difficult was actually something exciting and engaging that taught you to think beyond your objectives, plans, and targets and it is unlikely for you to learn about the process of becoming a car racer through video games.

Sitting in a zone of comfort is something that draws you back from accomplishing things rather than seeking them. When your body loses the drive to work and prefers to stay in comfort, it is something that draws you back from achieving things rather than chasing them. It's usually the great persons who never regard themselves as a spare; they understand that this is the only life they have, and they never view themselves as a spare to spend later and without regrets they spend their life in facing dangers.

CHAPTER TWENTY-ONE

Choosing and making decisions along with regrets

I feel that the 'WH' question style is the most effective way for us to learn about anything. Any query of WHY, I think, prompts a follow-up question of WHAT, piques your interest in HOW, prompts you to inquire about WHO, and eventually allows you to choose WHICH.

A choice is anything you make by selecting or choosing from accessible options, but a decision is something you make as the end result of available options, and it is sometimes the decision you adopt as conclusion.

In your life you come across various stages where you need to make decisions and choices to make a step ahead of your plans, it can you selecting a new outfit for your birthday of 2-3 choices, colours, styles etc, where as it can be your decision of your career, person you choosed to lived along with is something can be categorised under decisions. Here, choices can be single or multiple but whereas decision is meant to be known as the end or conculsion of deciding of what you exacly want.

Decisions doesn't need to make things work since for the reason and cause of you have decided, it can be an individual making a successful decision and an organization making the worst decision ever, so it depends with the way, your perspective in making out decisions you want to make out of.

Choices can be something considered as, you choosing or selecting something intended or randomly too among your available options. It doesn't require for choices to be right and not even for decisions to be right resulting to be right,

So here comes the term REGET,

- Does regret exist?, what actually a REGRET is?
- Which is considered to be REGRET?,
- Who feel or consider REGRET?

Regret is an emotional feeling that causes an individual to make a different decision in the past that may have resulted in something different from what you are experiencing now since the current conditions and events are unfriendly to you and distant from your expectations of your decisions.

Are you regretting a past decision or the unfavourable circumstances you are currently experiencing?

If it's the decision of yours in the past making you feel regret or feel bad for not choosing something else, your are considering yourself as TRASH BAG, any dcision made in the paast is made fromething out of your brain considering the facts and circumstances that were available to you on that particular second and you thought it might make a change and it might go wrong or fial based on circumstances which aren't under your control......So, rather than mourning the past, one of the finest pieces of advice ever offered is to focus on the future.

When I failed 2 subjects during the Diploma, it was the first ever I felt bad and then I made a thought process which involved the reasons for being sad and instead of knowing or realising the reasons I found nothing and I even then I failed the same subjects again and this this time I locked the door for sorrowness to not to enter and ended up watching a film.

So rather than ending in depression and things, it's the act you need to perform which results in taking over of things that made you sad and apart from the external factors that just help you, I believe it's your ownself that you are supposed to push or pull yourself away from terms of negative aspects that drag you down.

CHAPTER TWENTY-TWO

Grand Theft Auto: Vice City

"Of course, he looks like the suspect; that don't make him guilty.

You look like an idiot; that doesn't mean you are one." -Ken Rosenberg's

In 2012, my father took me to one of his colleagues' house and introduced me to his children, who are much older than me. We had a few casual conversations, and with time going off, one of them led me to his room and showed me his computer setup, which I adored, and it was then that I first encountered GTA III. He supported me in playing the game by addressing the rules and controls to play the game, and I used to act appropriately and guide to reach a location and accomplish my chores and objectives that I was intended to do; it was one of my finest experiences ever in aspect of playing video games.

Soon after, my father bought us a laptop, and after exploring the laptop's features, options, paint, word, and applications, it was then during vacation that I requested my father to install games to play, and after hundreds of requests from me and my brother, Sriram, it was then that my father agreed to install video games, Days later, he contacted others and received an installation with five games where one of them was GTA VICE CITY.

When I first observed the logo with a girl's cunning smile, I thought maybe it's a ladies game as of barbie girl and skipped of playing it but after playing the remaining games and got bored of and took a break from playing the games and after a while and I do remember the time I first ever launched the GTA VICE CITY application, it was around 8'o clock, when I launched the application, a gried of people appeared where one was them were smoking, a bike ride, helicopter, a boat and there appeared 3 options and then "START GAME".

It was first then the story started where three people were talking about something and a man was hanging in the background and, as usual, I clicked enter to skip the story and used to skip whenever stories appeared, I used to play missions, stealing cars from people, performing random stunts and kills, escaping from police whenever there was a chase by them while caught witnessing a theft, shooting random people, and doing some stuffy things to which and when it was then in my childhood where I never actually know the original reason of performing an act of murder, rescue and escape.

And the nostalgic days of playing vice city with installing applications where it does contain cheat codes and I used to write them on a paper and place it safe in a book and used to discuss it with my friend, Sarath chandra, and whenever he lost the paper of cheat chodes, I used to lend my paper of cheat codes and when it happens with me he lends his paper to me. My brother and I were so obsessed with the Vice City game that we would often call each other by the names of our favourite characters, yelling at one another, and my mother would stare at us from the corner of the room as if we were insane monkeys escaping from a nearby zoo.

There are several things I learned from GTA: Vice City, and a couple of them can be classified or mentioned as

- It's never about achieving peace at the end of a conflict or war between people; it's always about achieving victory.
- We do consider a prayer in our everyday life in terms of blessing our opponent to death, but it is their presence that makes your life fascinating and makes you conscious of every second.
- **Expect the unexpected,**Expect the unexpected. Just when you think you're secure sitting on the sofa watching Netflix with no worries, the fan revolving over your head falls on your skull, resulting in a cotton bandage wrapped over your face.
- **Jump when the car goes on fire,** When I play GTA and am driving a car and encounter numerous dashes to the walls, cars, and gunshots striking the car I'm riding in, which causes my car to blast off and lead me to attempt to get off the car and in rare cases I use cheatcodes like Aspirine to let the fire go off and escape from the cops while been in a chase Similar to the condition, when things are going to go horribly wrong, get out of the way and let them fly.
- **At the end of the day it's all about enjoying the day.**
- **You can buy anything and whatever you intent to buy and expand yourself.**
- **It's never about who you are or where you came from; rather, it's about what you can do in terms of deeds to stay alive.**
- **Money is only a means to an end; it is never the goal....** etc.., These are some of the things I learned while playing **Grand Theft Auto: Vice City.**

And the nostalgic days of playing vice city with installing applications where it does contain cheat codes and I used to write them on a paper and place it safe in a book and used to discuss it with my friend, Sarath chandra, and whenever he lost the paper of cheat chodes, I used to lend my paper of cheat codes and when it happens with me he lends his paper to me.

CHAPTER TWENTY-THREE

Phone

In my phone, I typed 90% of this book.

Now-a-days you doesn't actually require a huge setup and components to do or perform a certain task you want and need to, you might just need a phone or a tab,

My phone, on a personal level, has assisted me in learning a great deal about a wide range of topics. I'm amazed at how quickly the phone has taken over the globe in just a few years. I used to overhear people talking how we can talk to someone far away with just a phone call from here, and I used to see their responses to something called phones. Many folks I saw felt it was a magical or wizard tool for people who didn't know anything about phones.

During the era of the smartphones that went on craze for a certain time period, it was then from kids to adults in due time taught themselves about the phone with just a touch and indeed I saw certain people who considered the keypad phones as the healthyones, since they belived that buttons in the keypad used to help the fingers to perform certain exercise.

So, returning to the phone, Phone is something that may be viewed, in technical words, as a communications equipment at first, and then, with developments and ideas from engineers, it turned into something that utterly dominated the globe.

It was once when my friend and I went to someone he knew to clear his worries about technical words on his computer, and in the middle of the conversation, I asked him what it was all about, and he answered about the term he wanted to clarify his doubts regarding,

I simply googled related topics to learn about a few technical terms and his doubts about his computer's problem, and found a few answers, and after some time, we went to the technician, and my began to ask the technician about his doubts, and the technician began to give out a few explanations and had a list of components that needed to be changed, and in the meantime I explained my concerns to him and used a few technical terminology I was familiar with to find out the real issue and I had a list of alternatives that helped him reduce costs,

When my friend inquired when I had his information, I told him in the middle of the process, and he questioned how. and I said, "With the help of the internet,", So here, with the help of internet, I gained more knowledge from internet apart from my friend who is fond of using computers and the technician, who is fond of repairing or dealing with computer issues. Here, I believe the 3rd person, internet person, than the technician because he mentioned the steps of how it acts in the fault and the steps to perform during the fault.

Here, it might be someone from someplace working in a firm who, when asked a question or enquired about a query, replied it using a platform developed by someone else, thus the internet may be something like, I believe, a collection of ideas and information.

So here it's the phone that made a job or task of knowing about some information so easy and helped me in developing my knowledge, it can be people out there claiming, it's an addiction, I consider it as useless to term an habit as addiction.

From students to employees, from homeworks to EXEL sheets, people out there have an instant option in their hand which can be done time comparetively lower and ease in making progress of the task.

As a coin has two sides, so does the PHONE, which has two words that the majority considers to be a BAD element of innovation. I once saw an interview about cybercrimes, and when I saw a police officer addressing a kid in grade 8, he claimed himself as a Private Cybercrime Consultant, a term I had never heard of, and began to make money with some uploads done by him, in unauthorised or age restricted internet sites, and sharing them as a warning to people, and the fear of people's reputation is something he made money out of and When I first heard this tale and a few others related to it, I was taken aback, and it surprised me and made me think that the most ordinary people around us may go to great lengths to make a few things go smoothly for their choice of making things happen that are often labelled as BAD by society.

The thing that til surprises me about people of this kind is that, to make certain things, like money making in above example, the will of the people here is so strong that evantually made them to go far to any extent to satisfy their level of wants.

"If you look for perfection, you'll never be content"- Leo Tolstoy

Even then in considering the terms and apects of the negative shade and phase of the phone, I believe Good exists when evil or bad exists, so considering your term of being good or bad completely depend on your aspect of life, thought process and decision making.

CHAPTER TWENTY-FOUR

Fear of Fear

Fear doesn't actually have any form or kind of shape, it's just a feel. The ultimate reason that majority feel fear is something caused by the feel or tense of resulting in loss. Anything that makes an individual feel that particular decision he gonna make result in loss is something that make him feel the power of fear.

- It's always up to us to decide whether or not to make the act of breathing a survival act. Every time we take a breath, we have no idea when it will be our last; we approach the greatest limit of death and then return to life in our everyday lives, It might just be that you are exhaling your final breath, and because we aren't guaranteed the following breath, the last breath we live to make the decision to take a new breath is something done without fear.

It's the same as when we took our first breath when we joined the world; we didn't know what the term FEAR meant at the time, and it was gradually injected by the people, events, and circumstances around us into our brain, so fear is an act we are actually intended to act.

it's the action of breathing we have been doing from being an infant and this is something that haven't ever made us feel fear out. So, I believe, it's the act of habituating out our fear as an act of habit and doing out daily to make the act disappear, there's one of my quote, ignore the sense of injury and the injury itself disappear, as long as you give your time, attention, energy to the act and feel of fear it drains you out and the moment you believe it's inexisting, it's then inexistence.

Whenever I feel the fear, I consider myself and my surroundings as not reality and my senses are not reacting to them. Does it make any change?, my answer is YES, whenever I feel fear of things, I consider myself as artificial or inexistence and believe that anything that going around me is something is not reality and this help me to makes my senses go fine and I concentrate more, when it's a ghost film you understand that is not real, you concentrate on the story, plots, the effects, music and remaining technicals and ounderstand movie far better better than taking it with fear.

It can be different kinds of people watching ghost movies with different mentatilities and perspectives where I witnessed it once among my friends while watching a horror film where I observed different aspects as;

- One believe, watching ghost films or horror concepts in nights attract ghosts to and what if I encounter a ghost in mid-way to pee?
- One does believe, nothing like GHOST is in existence and it's stupidity to fear,
- One does make fun while watching the film and different perspectives of considering the term fear depends with different people who consider it as alike.

When you're driving down a dark and lonely road, it's easy to feel scared because you can't see what's beyond your headlight view, and when something like a dog crosses the road, it makes your heart skip a beat because there's something out there that happened without your knowledge or for which you weren't even prepared and the same car with a barrier on the border of the highway and clear visibility with street lights that helps in clear view of the road and you drive effectively without fear of surprise strikes and movements and the fear here it's comparatively super low while comparing it with dark and alone road.

When you can figure out the cause for you fear, it makes you feel a bit free since you know the cause for your fear.

When I feel FEAR of something I can't predict or know I search for reasons that helped my fear to develop and in instant I eliminate them and come up with thinking rather than worrying, I search for availability of what all I can do do to solve out an issue and if I found none, I take the result.

When you can write it down on a paper so that it can be you figuring out what's exactly making you to feel the fear can be terminated with the thought process of making a decision regarding in terms of developing a strategy or process of developing your self with your own defensive mechanisim or strinking out the fear and solving out your problems can make you feel free from FEAR.

CHAPTER TWENTY-FIVE

There are no great ones in this room....

The world we live in is like a room full of different people, each with their own set of thoughts, degrees of thinking, and IQs. So it is possible that you are constantly thinking about yourself, making decisions for yourself, and comparing yourself to yourself is a fantastic choice of idealogy for life to thrive and survive.

Imagine being the worst student in your class, and everyone from your teachers to your friends thinks you're useless, and they certainly believe you're useless to exist at times, with your friends ignoring and skipping your words, changing your topics and things, and it's something that can really hurt you and Imagine a day when you received the highest grade in your institution and now have everyone's focus on you. Even if you don't know how, once you do, you can simply realise that a student who studies well knows 2+2=4 and you know the same, therefore you both have the same knowledge to some level and you tend to make progress to collect knowledge and when your compared your ownself from one month back, previous week, previous day and even previous hour does help you in making progress.

Imagine you know something where none have the skill where you can make smething like origami out of papers and once made a rose and when you gifted it to a girl it does some form attention seekness to you by whole and that's when you are better than the others.

If someone speak out their idea for any particular task and if it goes well, here should we appreciate the idea or the person who gave the idea?, This question does have various answers in various perspectives and I do believe, in my own level of personal perspective, is that it's never the greatness of the person who provided or spoke out the idea or suggestion are completely based on the circumstances and material of choice that he/she had at that particular time.

So there's no one out there who is intended or called to be great or better, but it's all about the material of life, decision, viewpoint, and a few other elements that depend on that exact second of time to decide on the aspect of greatness, but it's not entirely accurate, but still it's never the perfection existing out there, the decisions you make on your own does help you to realize about yourself.

Any decision you take for yourself is one of the greatest things you do and apart from terms of considering the results that may occur in mean time after you take a decision is something you never have to bother about and work on your believed thought regardless of the output, maybe it might even lead you to something great out there which has been undiscovered and you can be the first ever person to discover something great.

CHAPTER TWENTY-SIX

Inexistence or In existence..?

There are two things in this world that assist us to think either rational or irrational and they are termed as Inexistence and In existence, Inexistence is the absence and inverse of the phrase existence, whereas existence is anything that has a presence in terms of several characteristics.

So what's about inexistence or in existence?

Imagine you being sad for scoring low grade in your academics and it's been something that feel as lost in your life and decided to end up everything and took a decision of taking things care next time and when actually performed it and when you observed that the results are something had a huge difference from past and you started to accept things happily and when you are about to sleep, there exist's a question from yourself to yourself, ARE YOU HAPPY?, and indeed you feel and say YES and at that instant when rised an another of WHY?, it can be your answer of your achivement or progress or developement from your past are something you address for your happiness and that moment you realised the actual intent of those questions in making you realize the answer for YES and worry you had once for NO.

Another example is that, I once witnessed a misunderstanding which took around 5 years for the one, who misunderstood, to realise with something called as truth or the facts of that particular moment. So the anger that once built up was later buired after the term of realisation.

Therefore the concern you previously had in existence is now something inexistence and the term angry that was once in existence is something inexistence now .... so the terms "worry" and "anger" meant to be in "existence" or "inexistence"?

Any emotion, I rationally believe, is inexistent non reality and only exists in the minds of individuals, thus instead of contemplating the phrases worry, concerns, wrath, sadness, and any other thoughts and emotions, I believe they are inexistent and irrelevant to the aspect of causes.

In my years of dealing with a variety of situations, I've always considered my presence to be a non-real aspect, and I've never considered any of my actions to be irrelevant to whether they went well or badly. The reason for this is that when you realise or pretend to believe you're a part of a simulation, you analyse what's going on around you instead of just proceeding thru it.

In final words, I thing I wanna say is that,

Believe yourself in terms of existence as inexistence, and b

Believe you are in existence in inexistence.

CHAPTER TWENTY-SEVEN

Couch-potato

In years of experience, there are two things that I understood from people and it's about their types, the one who work and the one who doesn't.

Majority of the people live their life staying on the couch which can be the cause with 2 things, fear and lack of making decision. We cannot claim them as failures neither as successful for reason of not having failures, I met many such potatos and still meeting people of such kind.

"More is lost by hesitation," I always love that one quote that greatly assisted me while thinking to make a decision and considered factors arund me, perspectives, requirements and many things and eventually took decisions so fast at times and never bothered about the result.

When an individual stay up in his couch watching useless stuff and let the time run ends up with regret of letting it. They don't even try to make an attempt to make a change from their routine life and end up in loosing many chances, oppurtunities and things.

The reasons and causes can vary depending on many factors, but when evaluating the bulk of causes, I believe it is their fear of losing that has always kept them back and never allowed them to make a decision outside of their safe or comfort zone.

Any loss of one's identity is referred to be a stepping stone or stairway built to alleviate fear. When you take things seriously, you are afraid of losing them; when you don't take yourself seriously, you don't even try to restrain yourself from acting regardless of the outcome.

There are certain things that surprise me to think about these people is that, they come up with an new alternative theory so fastly, once when I observed a person who always stay as a couch potato and once predicted about an upcoming film as a Flop and when the day arrived where the film actually blockbuster, he then started to claim that, there are no movie releases in near to this so people watched this and it just became hit in lucky,

Another example I witnessed is when I failed two topics in Diploma, one of my friends seemed to feel sorry for me, and I pretended to accept his sadness. He said things like, this time the question paper was so difficult that even I struggled to pass, and assure next time you crack it and When I somehow passed it out in the final year, his first reply was an unusual one in which he indicated that the government wants to pass out those who have taken supplementary examinations and want to make things easier. So they come up with an option so quickly and make sure they aren't mistaken. They never want to disgrace their words or never to get themselves being low around and among people.

The reason for these instances being written is to ensure that something about them is known. These couch-potatoes are individuals who speak so quickly and come up with a theory to ensure that they reach the other side of success. It's because they see themselves as better thinkers and decision-makers.

Since these kind of people can't make any decision in terms of progressive they always loved to stay down of ladder and start commenting on people who are on the way of reaching the sky, their ultimate target is to watch the opposite's fall and enjoy in one's failure.

That one term that always made me feel pity of these kind of people is that, they don't know that they are the actual couch-potatoes and they forever then compromise with the present and remain as useless,

So, it always be them, staying up back ending up their life by staying back too.